Contents

NUMBER JUGGLERS™

Preface for Parents and Teachers

Math can be a lot of fun. In fact, it can be downright exciting. Everyone knows something about math, and whatever you know is the best place to start. Little children know that if they are four on this birthday, they'll be more than four on their next birthday. They know that if they have three cookies and eat one, they'll have fewer than three cookies left. Studies show that from the time they are infants, humans have a basic understanding of quantity—of more and less—and that's what arithmetic is really all about.

Number Jugglers Math Games are designed to let players start where they feel comfortable. Because the games can adapt to all ages and all ability levels, the same game can be fun for a kindergartener, for a sixth-grader, and even for a college graduate. Siblings can enjoy playing them together at home. Parents can have fun playing them with their children. And at school, all the students in a class can be successful.

The level of skill needed for a particular game often depends simply on how many cards you use and how you set the rules.

For beginners who like to see the actual quantity of a number, the cards are marked with dots to count.

The dots also show the difference between odd numbers and even numbers, one of the most basic math concepts your children can learn.

Number Jugglers Math Cards do not include operation signs—the plus, minus, multiplication, and division signs that tell us what to do. We omitted them for a reason. When students see an operation sign, their brains seize on it. They see a plus sign and think addition. They see a multiplication sign and think multiplication. That limits their freedom to invent. In these games, we don't want to restrict your child's math creativity in any way. Looking at the numbers, children make whatever connections and relationships they can from their own store of math knowledge. The games are not threatening, because players start from where they feel comfortable. The games are good learning tools because they encourage players to make more and more complicated computations as they go along. There's fun and challenge for math whizzes and beginners alike.

The Introduction describes in simple terms everything you need to know to start playing these games. You might want to read through it with your children. After that, you'll be ready to begin climbing the Number Ladder, the first game in the book and one in which even the youngest players experience success.

Introduction

If you like math, these games are for you. And even if you think you'd rather be sitting in a tub of ice-cold water at the North Pole than playing math games, these games are for you, too. No matter what your age or your math skills, everyone can have fun with Number Jugglers Math Games. There's only one thing you need to know before you start to play. You need to know what this is:

=

Two short lines, one over the other, is a symbol we use to tell us that one thing equals another thing. It's called an EQUALS SIGN, and it's always used in a kind of number sentence called an EQUATION (ee-**kway**-zhun). Here is an example of an equation:

$$1 + 1 = 2$$

That number sentence says: one plus one equals two.

What does it mean to say that one thing is equal to another?

When I was younger, I didn't think it was fair if Mom gave my sister Harriet a piece of gum without giving me gum, too.

To make it equal, we both needed the same amount of gum.

That was a kind of equation. The amount of gum Harriet had was the same as the amount of gum I had. I was satisfied, and Harriet was happy, too, because she didn't have to give me any of her gum!

Now think about numbers. When I say "three," what comes to your mind? Do you count to three in your head? Do you picture three objects? Do you simply think of the number 3?

Whatever you think when I say "three," do you agree that the number 3 equals the number 3?

$$3 = 3$$

Is that confusing? Well, think of it this way: Does your nose equal your nose? I'm guessing that you probably said, "Of course my nose equals my nose." Things that exist equal themselves. The Greek philosopher Plato said that more than two thousand years ago, but even if he hadn't said it, we would have known it anyway. Some things you just know.

Numbers equal themselves, too. In fact, that is the simplest equation we can make, when both sides of the equals sign look exactly alike:

3 = 3

12 = 12

568 = 568

47,295,693 = 47,295,693

There are also many, many, many equations where the numbers around the equals sign look very different from each other. Here are some examples:

$$2 + 2 = 4$$

$$4 \times 2 = 7 + 1$$

$$5 \times 3 = 15$$

$$10 - 1 = 9$$

$$3 - 2 = 5 - 4$$

These number sentences are equations, too, because they follow the very important RULE OF EQUATIONS:

Whatever is on the left side of the equation must equal the SAME AMOUNT as whatever is on the right side of the equation.

Let's check one out to see how it works:

$$3 - 2 = 5 - 4$$

On the left side of the equals sign we have 3 – 2. That says, three take away two.

By the way, some people say minus when they read this sign (–). "Minus" means the same thing as "take away." So you could say, three minus two.

What happens when you take two things away from three things?

That's right. You're left with one.

On the right side of the equals sign we have 5 – 4. That says five take away (or minus) four.

What happens when you take four things away from five things?

That's right. You're left with one.

Do you agree that one equals one?

YES! So 3 – 2 equals 5 – 4 because:

$$3 - 2 = 1 \quad \text{and} \quad 5 - 4 = 1$$

$$1 = 1$$

Make some equations of your own. Try some in your head first. Say them out loud.

Now take out your deck of Number Jugglers Math Cards. Shuffle the deck and deal yourself ten cards. If you get too many of one number, you can trade them in for other numbers. Lay the cards number-side-up on the table or floor in front of you. Look them over. Can you make any equations with the numbers on your cards? Move the cards around to give yourself some ideas.

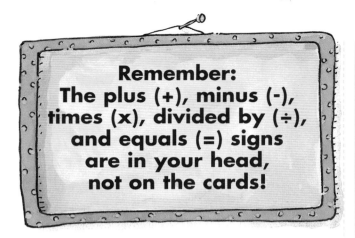

Remember:
The plus (+), minus (-),
times (x), divided by (÷),
and equals (=) signs
are in your head,
not on the cards!

A Note About the Game Cards

The instructions to each game tell you how many cards you need to play that game.

When the cards are dealt, sometimes players find themselves with four 3 cards, or three 0 cards, or five 9 cards.

If you end up with more than two cards of the same number, you are allowed to trade in the extras for other cards.

In the case of 0 cards, the rule is even more flexible. Players who receive more than ONE 0 card may trade in all but one 0 card for new cards.

Now that you know about equations, you're ready to play the games.

HAVE FUN!

The Number Ladder Game

Single players or teams try to climb the ladder as high as possible. Use your cards to make equations that equal the number of each rung. Write your equation on the rung. You can keep drawing more ladders if you need to, or use a big roll of paper to keep the same ladder going.

How to Play

1 Each player or team draws a ladder on a piece of paper. Label the first rung 1, the second 2, the third 3, and so on. As you play you can keep adding rungs.

2 Shuffle the cards and deal each player or team ten cards. Use these same ten cards over and over.

3 If you have a 1 card, write 1 on the first rung of your ladder. If you don't have a 1 card, make an equation that equals 1 by adding, subtracting, multiplying, or dividing the numbers on your cards. Write your equation on the first rung.

4 Now go to the second rung. If you have a 2 card, write 2 on the second rung of your ladder. If you don't have a 2 card, use your cards to make an equation that equals 2 and write that on the second rung. Next, find or make 3, 4, 5, etc. Write your equations on each rung.

5 You may NOT put two cards together to make a higher number. For example, a 3 card and a 4 card DO NOT make 34 or 43.

6 Keep climbing the ladder, one rung at a time, until you can't make an equation that equals the next rung's number. The highest rung you climb to is your score.

7 Each card may be used only ONCE in an equation, but you may use all your cards again for the next equation.

8 You can make complicated equations or simple ones. You only need to use your cards to make the left side of the equation. The right side of the equation is the number of the rung. **See note for very young players on page 16.**

Equation	Rung
$4 \times 2 + (3 - 2)$	9
4×2	8
$3 + 4$	7
3×2	6
$3 + 2$	5
4	4
3	3
2	2
$3 - 2$	1

Number Ladder Challenges

(for intermediate and advanced players)

For these games, remove the zero cards from the Number Jugglers deck. Use only the cards numbered from 1 to 10.

Challenge #1: Climb the number ladder using only six cards. You may use each card only once per equation, but you may use all your cards again for the next equation.

Challenge #2: Climb the number ladder using only five cards.

Challenge #3: Climb the number ladder using only four cards.

Super Challenge: Climb the number ladder using only five cards. You MUST USE ALL FIVE CARDS for each equation.

NOTE: Very young players may need help drawing their ladders and writing their equations. Or you may choose to play the game without writing anything down. Players can say their equations out loud. It's fun for younger children to play in teams of three or four. They can point to the numbers as they climb the rungs. When they get to a rung for which they have to make an equation, they can collaborate. For example, you can say: "Uh-oh. We don't have a 6. Is there any way we can get to rung 6?" Then let them figure it out themselves without adult input. When they get stuck, that's their score.

That's Odd!

Have you ever noticed that if you and your friend have four cookies, it's easy to divide them up between you?

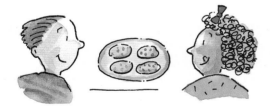

You each get two cookies.

But if you and your friend have five cookies, it's harder to divide them up. You each get two cookies and there's one left over.

Well, we share by breaking it in half.

Right. But what if you had something you couldn't break in half, like a balloon? What would happen then?

We'd have one left over.

That's right, because five is not an even number.

Numbers that can be divided into two equal groups are called even numbers.

When we count by two's we name all the even numbers.

2	4	6	8	10
12	14	16	18	20
22	24	26	28	30

and so on, and on, and on, and on. As you can see, even numbers all end in a 2, a 4, a 6, an 8, or a zero.

All the other numbers are called odd numbers, because when you try to divide them into two equal groups, you will always end up with one left over.

What numbers do you think odd numbers end in?

Look at your Number Jugglers Math Cards and see if you can tell just from

the dots which are the odd numbers.

What about zero? Is zero an odd or an even number?

That's right. Zero can't be divided.

I don't think it's either one. Because zero is no number at all. You can't divide zero into any groups!

But numbers that end in zero can be divided. All numbers that end in zero are even numbers, except for zero itself.

The Odd and Even Game

For two players. Players take turns guessing whether cards in the deck will be odd or even.

How to Play

1 Remove the 0 cards from the deck.

2 Each player picks a card. The person with the lowest number goes first. Put the cards back into the deck and shuffle it.

3 Place the deck, number-side-down, in a pile in the middle. Whoever goes first guesses whether the top card is odd or even. If you guess right, you keep the card and take another turn guessing. If you guess wrong, you give the card to the other player, and it becomes his turn.

4 Keep playing until there are no more cards left in the middle pile. Count the cards you have kept. Each card is worth 2 points. The player with the most points wins.

QUESTION

When the 0's are removed, there are 74 cards in the Number Jugglers deck. Could the game end up in a tie?

Yes

The Golden Rule of Equations

Tricks & Ideas for Getting More Points

Do unto one side as you do unto the other!

One of the best things about equations is that you can play around with them without ruining them, just as long as you keep this in mind:

If you do something that changes the total of one side of an equation, you must make an equivalent change to the other side.

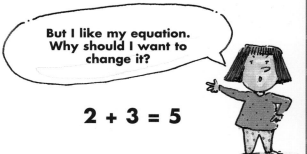

But I like my equation. Why should I want to change it?

2 + 3 = 5

If you want to use more cards and get more points, you can do this:

2 + 3 + 1 = 5 + 2 − 1

Remember this rule when you play **The Equation Game** on the next page.

The Equation Game

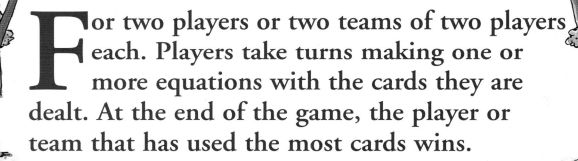

For two players or two teams of two players each. Players take turns making one or more equations with the cards they are dealt. At the end of the game, the player or team that has used the most cards wins.

How to Play

1 Decide if you want to have a time limit for each turn. Then, each player or team picks one card from the deck. The player who draws the highest card goes first.

2 Shuffle the deck and deal the first player ten cards. Lay your cards face up in front of you, and move them around to make one long equation or several shorter equations.

3 You must have the correct cards for *both* sides of the equation. For example, to make the equation

$$2 \times 3 = 4 + 2$$

you must have a 2, a 3, a 4, and another 2 card.

4 You may add, subtract, multiply, or divide your numbers, but you may

NOT put two cards next to each other to create a higher number. For example: a 4 card and a 5 card do not make 45 or 54.

5 Use as many of your cards as you can in each turn. Keep the cards you use and store them in a separate pile to count at the end of the game. Return unused cards to the deck.

6 After the first player or team is finished, deal ten cards to the second player. The second player makes equations with his cards and keeps the cards he uses in a separate pile. Unused cards are returned to the deck.

7 Take turns, back and forth, until the players or teams have had an equal number of turns and there are not enough cards left in the deck to continue playing.

8 Count your cards. The player or team with the most cards wins the game.

The Make a Number Game

For one to six players. Players will need pencils and paper, a die or spinner, and a timer or stopwatch. Players use their cards to make as many equations as they can in a given amount of time. The player who makes the most equations wins the game.

How to Play

1 Two minutes is generally long enough. But you can decide to make it longer if you wish.

2 Each player receives ten cards and lays them out, number-side-up.

3 Someone rolls the die, spins the spinner, or calls out a number. This number is the goal. Say it out loud so everyone can hear. Begin timing from that point.

4 Using the numbers on your cards, make as many equations as you can to equal the goal number. You may use each card only once per equation, but you may use all your cards again for the next equation.

5 Example: Say the goal number is 4. Look at your cards and make an equation to equal 4. If you have a 6 and a 2, write down $6 - 2 = 4$. Keep making equations and writing them down until your time is up.

6 When the time is up, count the number of CORRECT equations you have made. Each correct equation is worth two points. The person with the most points wins the game.

Challenge: Deal each player only six cards to use for equations. Each correct equation is worth five points.

The Win It! Game

(for intermediate players)

For two to five players. The more people playing, the more fun it is.

How to Play

1 Remove the 0 cards from the deck and shuffle the cards that remain. Deal five cards to each player. Lay them number-side-up in front of you. These are the cards players use to make their equations.

2 Place the rest of the cards in a pile in the middle, number-side-down. All players must sit so they can reach the cards in the middle.

3 When everyone is ready, someone turns over the card on top of the pile. That becomes the WIN card. Use your cards to try to make an equation that equals the WIN card.

4 You must use at least TWO of your cards to make your equation. You may add, subtract, multiply, or divide the numbers on your cards. You may use each of your cards only once per round. All five cards may be used again in the next round.

5 The first player to make an equation slaps the WIN card and says, "Win It!" He must say his winning equation to the others. If it is correct, he takes the WIN card to keep in a separate pile.

6 You may not slap the pile until you are sure of your equation. Any player who slaps the pile early loses that turn.

7 Each round begins by turning over the next WIN card. The game is over when there are no more cards left in the middle. Each WIN card is worth one point. Whoever has the most points is the winner.

Challenge: Players receive six cards each. Divide the rest of the cards into two middle piles, numbers down. Turn both top cards over and multiply them together to make the WIN number. Players must use at least THREE cards to make the WIN equation. The first person to do so calls "Win It!" and slaps the pile. If the equation is correct, the player keeps both WIN cards.

Use 1 for More Fun

Let's say you have four pieces of candy.

What happens if you multiply that group of four candies by 2?

You get eight candies. Four pieces of candy two times.

4 x 2 = 8

What happens if you multiply that group of four candies by 3?

You have twelve pieces of candy.

4 x 3 = 12

Now, what happens when you multiply your group of four candies by 1? What do you have then?

WHAT???! You have only those same four candies!

Why? Doesn't multiplying make more?

Only sometimes. When you multiply by 1, you only get to take that group of four candies ONE time, and that means you end up with the same amount you started with.

4 x 1 = 4

Now, that fact can be very important to anyone who wants to play the games in this book, because in some of the games, it's good to use as many cards as you can.

So?

So if you have a 1 card or can make a 1, you can multiply any number by that 1 and not change the value of your equation at all. Which means you use more cards and get more points!

I don't get it!

Well, think about it this way. Say you make this equation:

3 x 2 = 6

How many cards does that give you?

You use three cards: the 3, the 2, and the 6. Now, what if you made the equation like this:

$$3 \times 2 = 6 \times 1$$

It still works, because multiplying by 1 doesn't change the value of the number.

And now instead of getting only three cards, you get to keep four cards, which means another point for you.

If you multiplied the numbers on both sides of the equation by 1, would it still work?

$$3 \times 2 \times 1 = 6 \times 1$$

Yes!

Even if you don't have any 1 cards, you can make 1.

Make 1 by subtracting.

Subtracting means to take away. Can you think of a way to make 1 out of a 5 card and a 4 card?

You can subtract: 5 take away 4 equals 1.

$$5 - 4 = 1$$

What would you have to take away from 8 to make 1?

8 take away 7 equals 1.

$$8 - 7 = 1$$

Make 1 by dividing.

You can also make 1 by dividing.

But I don't know how to divide.

I bet you do! Check out these four dogs.

Divide them into groups of two each. How many groups do you have?

There are two groups of two dogs.

4 ÷ 2 = 2

You just divided. Dividing is finding out how many groups of one number are in another number.

Now, ask yourself, how many groups of four are in 4?

When you divide 4 into 4, you have only enough to make one group. Four goes into itself only one time.

4 ÷ 4 = 1

The fact is, whenever you divide any number into itself, the answer is always going to come out 1.

2 ÷ 2 = 1
6 ÷ 6 = 1
20 ÷ 20 = 1
100 ÷ 100 = 1

That's how you make 1 by dividing.

Now you might want to try playing The Equation Game again using the tricks you just learned to win more cards.

The Make 10 Game

For two players or two teams. Each player or team tries to use as many cards as possible to make a single equation that equals 10. At the end of the game, the player or team with the most cards wins.

How to Play

1 Decide if you want a time limit. Two minutes per turn is about right. Decide which player or team goes first by drawing a card from the deck. Whoever draws the highest card goes first.

2 Each player gets ten cards per turn. Lay the cards number-side-up in front of you.

3 Try to find a way to make your numbers equal 10. Make only ONE equation. You may add, subtract, multiply, or divide the numbers on your cards.

4 Use your cards for the left side of the equation only. Don't use any cards for the right side of the equation.

5 In making your equation, use as many cards as you can. For example:

(6 + 4 - 3 - 2) x 2 uses five cards. But 5 + 5 uses only two cards.

6 You may use each card ONLY ONCE in your equation.

7 KEEP all the cards you use. Return the cards you don't use to the deck.

Keep playing back and forth until players have had an equal number of turns and there are not enough cards left in the deck to continue playing.

8 Players count the cards they have kept. Each card is worth one point. The player with the most points wins the game.

Be a Number Doctor

 Adding (+), subtracting (−), multiplying (×), and dividing (÷) are called OPERATIONS. Whenever you add, subtract, multiply, or divide numbers, you are performing a mathematical operation, which means you become a NUMBER DOCTOR!

Doctor, I need this 10 changed into a 6. Can you do it?

Let me think... Yes! We'll subtract 4 from it. That will be $20 please.

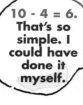

10 − 4 = 6. That's so simple. I could have done it myself.

Oh, so you want something a little more exciting, do you? Well, how about this:

10 ÷ 5 + 4 = 6

Elegant, isn't it? $40 please.

Isn't that a lot of money for just a two-step operation?

Well, for only $10 more, I will perform major surgery on that 10. What numbers can you give me to work with?

Come with me to the operating table and I'll show you.

Let's go through it together.
10 + 1 − 3 ÷ 2 × 3 − 2 ÷ 5 + 8 − 4 = 6

First add 1 to 10:
Then take away 3:
Next, divide by 2:
Then multiply by 3:
Subtract 2:
Then divide by 5:
Now add 8:
And finally, subtract 4:

$$10 + 1 = 11$$
$$11 - 3 = 8$$
$$8 \div 2 = 4$$
$$4 \times 3 = 12$$
$$12 - 2 = 10$$
$$10 \div 5 = 2$$
$$2 + 8 = 10$$
$$10 - 4 = 6$$

Well that's the way Number Doctors perform all their operations: one step at a time!

It's so easy when you do it that way!

You can be the Number Doctor by playing The Operation Game on page 38.

Parentheses

(pah-**ren**-theh-sees)

These things ( ) are called parentheses, and they are used a lot in math equations. They tell us what operations have to be performed FIRST.

For example, take 6 − (3 + 3) = 0

$$6 - (3 + 3) = 0$$

What if we wrote that without the parentheses:

6 − 3 + 3

Would that still equal 0?

NO! It wouldn't equal 0 because you would read the equation this way:

6 minus 3, plus 3.

That equals 6, not 0, because 6 minus 3 leaves 3 left over. Then you still have another 3 to add, and 3 plus 3 equals 6.

In this equation we put parentheses around the 3 + 3:

6 − (3 + 3) = 0

That way we know to add 3 + 3 BEFORE we subtract it from 6. Only then will the equation be true. Look at these examples:

4 x 1 + 1 = 5
4 x (1 + 1) = 8

Play **The One Equals One Game** on page 40 to see how easy it is to use parentheses.

The Operation Game

For two teams of one, two, or three players each. Each team needs a pencil and paper. The object is to make an equation that begins with a START card and ends up equaling a FINISH card. Points are awarded for the operations used in the equation. The team with the equation that earns the most points wins the game.

How to Play

1 Remove the 0 cards from the deck. Shuffle the deck and deal ten cards to each team. Lay your cards number-side-up. Each team picks one card to be the START card and one to be the FINISH card. The START card goes on the left and the FINISH card on the right.

2 Each team makes one equation that begins with their START card and ends up equaling their FINISH card.

3 Write your equation down, showing all operation signs. Points are awarded as follows:

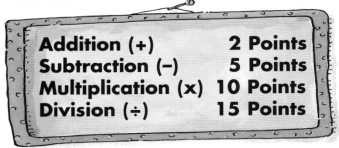

Addition (+)	**2 Points**
Subtraction (–)	**5 Points**
Multiplication (x)	**10 Points**
Division (÷)	**15 Points**

4 Check your equation to make sure it works. Then exchange equations with the other team. If the other team finds that your equation is incorrect, fix it and take 10 points off your score.

5 Add up your points. The team whose equation earns the most points wins the game.

NOTE: Beginning math players may want to use only plus and minus signs. In that case, make each plus sign (+) worth 5 points, and each minus sign (–) worth 10 points.

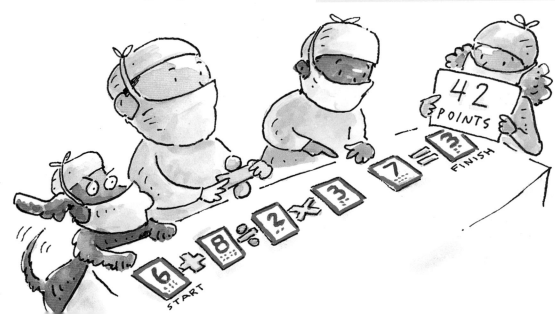

The One Equals One Game

(for intermediate and advanced players)

The purpose of this game is to come up with an equation that equals 1, using parentheses and as many of your cards as you can. Players need pencils and paper.

How to Play

1 Shuffle the deck and deal ten cards to each player or team, number-side-up.

2 Look over your cards. Group the numbers, using parentheses, and make an equation in which both sides equal 1.

3 You receive 2 points for every card you use and 5 points for every set of parentheses you use.

For example, John has these cards:

He uses seven cards this way:

$$(\boxed{7} - \boxed{6}) \times \boxed{!} = (\boxed{3} \times \boxed{3}) - (\boxed{4} + \boxed{4})$$

$$1 \times 1 = 9 - 8$$

$$1 = 1$$

John uses three sets of parentheses at 5 points each: $3 \times 5 = 15$ points.

He uses seven cards at 2 points each: $7 \times 2 = 14$ points.

15 points + 14 points = 29 points. John gets 29 points for his equation.

4 Once you have figured out your equation, write it down and count up your points. Then pass your paper to your opponent to check.

5 If your equation is correct, you keep your points. If your equation is incorrect, correct it and take 10 points off your score.

The Nine-Line Phenomenon

Players form a "nine line" by placing cards next to each other that will equal 9 when added together. Players will need pencil and paper.

How to Play

1 Remove all the 10 cards from the Number Jugglers deck. Arrange the remaining cards into piles. All the 0's in one pile, all the 1's in another pile, all the 2's in another pile, and so on. Pick your numbers from these piles.

2 Make a column of cards starting with 9 at the top; place 8 under it; 7 under that; 6 under 7; and so on down to 1. Put a 0 card under the 1. This is the right-hand column.

3 Now, to choose cards for the left-hand column, pick cards that when added to the right-hand column equal 9. For example, what would you add to 8 to make 9? 1. So put a 1 card on the left of the 8 card.

4 Keep going until the left-hand column is complete and all the double numbers added together equal 9.

5 Look at the columns you have made. Do you notice anything interesting about them?

6 Now write down your nines multiplication table, starting with 1×9 and ending with 10×9. You get 10 points for each one you know.

Times Square

Look over Times Square on the next page. Can you see how it works? It's all about multiplication—one number TIMES another number.

Each column going down is the multiplication table for the number at the top. Each row going across is the multiplication table for the number at the left. When you want to multiply, put one index finger on one number at the top and your other index finger on another number at the left, and pull your fingers together down and across the squares until they meet. That number is the answer to the problem.

For example,

8 x 7 = ?

Put a finger of one hand on 8 at the top. Put a finger of the other hand on 7 on the left. Pull the 8 finger down and the 7 finger across until they meet at 56.

8 x 7 = 56.

1	2	3	4	5	6	7	8	9	10
2	4	6	8	10	12	14	16	18	20
3	6	9	12	15	18	21	24	27	30
4	8	12	16	20	24	28	32	36	40
5	10	15	20	25	30	35	40	45	50
6	12	18	24	30	36	42	48	54	60
7	14	21	28	35	42	49	56	63	70
8	16	24	32	40	48	56	64	72	80
9	18	27	36	45	54	63	72	81	90
10	20	30	40	50	60	70	80	90	100

The Times Square Game

For two players or two teams. Players draw cards from the deck and multiply them together. When their answers are correct, players keep the cards they have multiplied. At the end of the game, the team with the most cards wins.

How to Play

1 Remove the 0 cards from the deck.

2 Each player or team picks a number from the deck. The highest number goes first.

3 Shuffle the deck and divide it into two even piles. Place the piles in the middle, number-side-down. The first player or team turns over the top card from each pile and multiplies these two numbers together.

4 If the answer is correct, the player keeps the two cards. If not, the player returns the cards to the bottom of the deck.

5 The second player or team picks the top card from each pile and multiplies the two together. If the answer is correct, the player keeps the cards. If not, the cards are returned and the first player or team goes again.

6 Play back and forth until all the cards have been won.

7 The Times Square on page 45 may be consulted to see if an answer is correct or incorrect, but it may not be used to help players get their answers.

8 At the end of the game, both teams count their cards. The team with the most cards wins the game.

The Golden Rule Game

For two players or two teams. One player makes an equation, the other adds cards to the equation to make a new equation, without altering the operation of the equation. Players who successfully create new equations get to keep the cards. Whoever has the most cards at the end of the game wins.

How to Play

1 Players pick a card from the deck to see who goes first. The player or team with the highest card goes first.

2 Deal ten cards, number-side-up, to the player or team that goes first.

3 The first player looks over the cards and makes a simple equation. She turns the cards to face her opponent (see illustration) and gives her opponent the rest of the cards.

4 The operations of this original equation may not be altered. For example, if the original equation says 4 + 1 = 5, the + sign may not be altered to make it say $4 \div 1$ or 4×1 or $4 - 1$.

5 The second player operates on the original equation, using as many of the remaining cards as he can. He may change one or both sides of the original equation—as long as when he is finished, the left side of his equation equals the right side.

6 If the new equation works, the second player keeps all the cards used. If the equation does not work, the first player

corrects it and keeps the cards. All cards that weren't used in the equation are returned to the bottom of the deck.

7 Deal ten new cards and play the next round. This time, the second player makes a simple equation and the first player adds cards to it.

8 Take turns back and forth until both players have had an equal number of turns and there are not enough cards left to continue playing.

9 Then count the cards you have kept. The player with the most cards wins the game.

Use Zero Without Fear-O

What would happen if you had three kids and you took away zero kids?

You'd still have three kids because you took NOTHING away.

What would happen if you had three kids and you added zero kids?

You'd still have the same three kids because you added NOTHING to the group.

When you make equations, you can ADD or SUBTRACT 0 to either side, and it won't change the equation either.

Let's make an equation:

$6 + 1 = 7$

Now add 0 and see what happens.

It still equals 7 because adding 0 doesn't change anything.

Subtract 0 from the equation and see what that does.

The equation still equals 7!

When you add 0 to or subtract 0 from your equations, it doesn't change the value at all. (This trick DOES NOT work with multiplying or dividing by 0. Think about why that might be.)

If you're playing a game that gives points for the number of cards you use, you can get more points by adding or subtracting 0 from your equation and using more cards.

But how can I add 0 if I don't have any 0 cards in my hand?

Use the cards you do have to MAKE 0.

The Deal Six Challenge Game

(for intermediate and advanced players)

For two players or two teams. Teams work best when there are no more than two or three players on each. Players challenge each other to make equations with their cards to equal a specific number between 1 and 100. The player or team that uses the most cards wins.

How to Play

1 Remove the 0 cards from the deck and shuffle the cards. Deal six cards to each player. Keep your cards secret until the challenge is made.

2 Decide who will challenge first.

The first player picks a number between 1 and 100 and says: "I challenge you to make . . ." (any number you choose). This is the challenge number.

3 The second player uses her cards to try to make an equation to equal the challenge number.

4 Each card may be used only once in the equation.

5 Each card you use is worth one point. Keep the cards you have used in a separate pile. Return unused cards to the bottom of the deck.

6 Reverse roles so that the second player challenges the first player to make a number between 1 and 100.

7 If you cannot make the challenge number in your turn, you must return all your cards to the deck and receive no points for that turn.

8 Keep taking turns, reshuffling the deck and dealing six new cards for each round.

9 After each side has had five turns, count the cards you have kept. The team with the most cards wins the game.

It's Digit-al!

You probably know that 10 is more than 9. In fact, 10 is the next number up when you count by ones, so 10 is exactly one more than 9.

$$9 + 1 = 10$$

Now that's interesting, because 9 is only one digit and 1 is only one digit, but when you add them together you get 10, which is two digits.

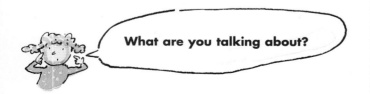

What are you talking about?

I'm talking about the way we write numbers. We call our number symbols DIGITS. And we have only ten of them: 0, 1, 2, 3, 4, 5, 6, 7, 8, 9. When we get to 9, we can't write any higher numbers unless we do something different.

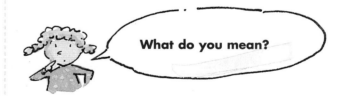

What do you mean?

Well, it's like using the alphabet to write words. There are only twenty-six letters in the English alphabet, but we have a lot more than twenty-six words in our dictionaries. That's because we put those twenty-six letters together in different combinations to make words. We combine letters to make words. To make numbers, we combine digits. But we can't just put digits together any which way and hope for the best. We need a method. And some brilliant Arab mathematicians figured out the method a long time ago. They needed only one thing to make their method work:

Columns.

In arithmetic, columns tell us how much each digit is worth. Every digit needs to be in a column so we know what amount it stands for.

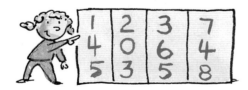

Each column has a name, and its name gives us the information we need. The first column on the right is called the **ones** column. It tells us how many single things we are talking about. So if there's a 5 in the first column, we know we are talking about five things.

5 x 1 = 5

Moving to the left, the second column is the **tens** column (ten times more than the ones column). A 5 in the tens column isn't just 5. It's 5 tens, which equals 50.

5 x 10 = 50

By combining the digits, we can make the two-digit number 55.

That would be a 5 in the tens column and a 5 in the ones column:

5 tens equals 50.

5 ones equals 5.

Put them together and we have 50 + 5, or 55

What's the highest two-digit number we can make?

I know. 99. You can't go higher than 9 in any column.

That's right. It's 99. That's 9 ones and 9 tens. After 99 you move to another column.

The hundreds column!

Moving to the left again, the next column is the **hundreds** column. It's ten times more than the tens column. It tells us how many hundreds we are talking about. A 5 in the hundreds column tells us we have 5 hundreds.

5 x 100 = 500

The next column to the left is ten times more than the hundreds column. It's the **thousands** column. It tells us how many thousands we have. A 5 in the thousands column means 5000.

5 x 1000 = 5000

If we had 5's in all four columns, we would have the number 5555:

5000 + 500 + 50 + 5

Five thousand, five hundred, fifty-five.

After the thousands column there is the **ten thousands** column and then the **hundred thousands** column. Next is the **millions** column. The millions column is the seventh column.

You might think it all sounds very complicated, but it really isn't complicated at all, because each set of three columns is arranged the same way:

Ones, tens, and hundreds
One thousands, ten thousands, hundred thousands
One millions, ten millions, hundred millions
One billions, ten billions, hundred billions
One trillions, ten trillions, hundred trillions

And so on and on and on and on and on. Columns can go on forever.

The Column Game

(for intermediate players)

For two players or two teams. Players use five cards to make a number. The die is rolled to see whether the highest number or the lowest number wins. Players will need a die cube.

1 Remove the 10 cards from the deck. NOTE: IN THIS GAME YOU USE YOUR CARDS AS DIGITS.

2 Shuffle the deck and deal five cards to each player or team. Lay cards number-side-up in front of you.

3 Roll the die. An even number means: arrange your cards into the highest number you can make. An odd number means: arrange your cards into the lowest number you can make.

4 Then roll the die again. If it's even, the player or team with the higher number wins both players' or teams' cards. If it's odd, the player or team with the lower number wins both players' or teams' cards.

5 Keep playing until there are no longer enough cards left for another turn.

6 Players count the cards they have taken. The player or team with the most cards wins the game.

Oh, Momma, I Need a Comma

You can probably imagine that when you have really, really, really long numbers, they can get pretty hard to read.

Take this one, for example:

85790504302

To help us read long numbers, we use the Comma Trick. It's a very simple trick. To remember it, just think of this poem:

Start on the right and count left three,

That's where the comma's supposed to be.

Got lots of digits? Commas work fine

To break them up, three at a time.

Thanks to the comma, no number's too long,

Just count left three, and you'll never be wrong.

Use the Comma Trick for every number that has more than three columns.

Here's how you do it: Start counting from the **ones** column on the right side of the number. Count three columns to the left. Then, put in a comma to separate the **hundreds** column from the **thousands** column.

If the number is longer than six columns, count to the left three more columns and put in another comma. That one separates the **hundred thousands** column from the **millions** column.

If the number is bigger than **millions**, continue counting to the left three more and put another comma in there, too. It's always the same. Count three to the left and put in a comma to separate the columns.

Put commas in

85790504302

and presto! It becomes

85,790,504,302

Eighty-five billion, seven hundred ninety million, five hundred four thousand, three hundred two.

Thanks, Mom!

The Counting Game

For one or two players. See how far you can count in a minute, then multiply to figure out how far you could count in ten minutes and how far in an hour.

How to Play

1 Time yourself with a stopwatch, or the second hand of a regular watch, and see how far you can count in one minute.

2 Time your friend and see how far he or she can count in a minute.

3 Now try to figure out how far you'd each be able to count in ten minutes.

...1,240...1,241...1,242...1,243...1,244...

So Many Numbers, So Little Time

Numbers go on forever. With the help of commas we can read very, very, very long numbers. But that doesn't mean we can count to them. It would take someone more than an average lifetime just to count to a billion. Not to mention how skinny and tired that person would be, since he or she wouldn't be able to take any time out to eat, or sleep, or have a life.

...999,999,999...1,000,000,000

4 Make that number with the Number Jugglers cards.

5 Make commas out of paper clips or other small objects. Insert commas into your number at the right spots (every three columns).

6 Next, try to figure out how far you'd each be able to count in one hour. Make that number with your cards.

The Skyscraper Game

(for intermediate and advanced players)

Two players or teams construct a skyscraper out of cards by making equations to equal the floor numbers. You will need paper, pencils, and a large playing space, such as the floor or a long table.

1 Decide if you want a time limit per turn. Players pick a card from the deck. The player with the lower number goes first.

2 Deal the first player ten cards, number-side-up. Make an equation to equal 1 and lay it down to construct the first floor. Then try to make an equation

to equal 2, and lay it down above the first equation. Continue making equations to construct each floor until you can't make the next number.

3 Keep score as follows: For each floor you build, multiply the number of cards used by the floor number (1 for the first floor, 2 for the second floor, etc.). Write your score on the paper.

4 Any cards you do not use in a turn are kept in a "personal game pile," which may be used in your next turn along with the ten new cards you are dealt.

5 The second player is dealt ten cards to continue. Starting where the first player left off, he makes an equation to equal the next floor number and lays it down. He continues building the skyscraper until he can't make the next floor number. Unused cards are kept in his personal game pile.

6 Each player or team has four turns. Cards still remaining in the deck are divided equally between players for the final round. At the end, players add up their points. The one with the most points wins the game.

The Make 100 Game

(for intermediate and advanced players)

For two to four players. You need paper and a pencil for each player to keep score. Use your cards to make equations to equal 100.

How to Play

1 Remove the 0 cards and shuffle the deck. Deal each player five cards, number-side down. Turn over your cards all at the same moment.

2 Players have 30 seconds to make an equation that equals 100. You may NOT put two cards together to make a higher number. For example, a 3 card and a 4 card DO NOT make 34 or 43.

3 You may add, subtract, multiply, or divide the numbers on your cards. You may also use your card numbers as exponents:

$$5^2 = 25$$

4 The player who makes 100 using the most cards gets one point.

5 If no one makes 100 exactly, the person who comes closest wins the point.

6 In case of a tie, the person who has used the most cards in his equation wins the point. If a tie persists, tying players are each awarded one point.

7 Players return their cards to the deck, which is reshuffled, and five new cards are dealt to each player for the next round.

8 The first player to get five points wins the game.

$$(8 \times 10) + (4 \times 5) =$$

$$(9 \times 9) + (3 \times 2) + 10$$

$$3 \times 10 \div 2 \times 7 - 5$$

100

The Importance of Being Zero

Okay. Let's say I tell you I have 8.

That's nice, you might say, thinking I mean plain old 8.

But what if I tell you my 8 is in the millions column—8,000,000?

Oh, that's different, you might say.

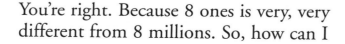

You're right. Because 8 ones is very, very different from 8 millions. So, how can I show you that I have 8 millions and not just 8 ones?

By putting the 8 in the seventh column, the millions column.

Exactly!

Uh-oh. You need something to fill up the other columns.

That's right. To make 8 into 8 million, you put 8 in the millions column, but you also have to put 0 in the other columns. That way, everyone knows you're talking about 8,000,000 and not just plain old 8.

Zero is a column marker. It lets us know the column is there even when there isn't any other digit in it. Zero says: This column has nothing in it.

Now, let's say we have one hundred marbles and someone gives us five more marbles. How can we write one hundred five marbles?

105

That says one hundred five.
There's 1 hundred, 0 tens, and 5 ones.

So, whenever we don't have any other digit in a particular column, we mark it with a 0.

Ten Makes It Easy

Have you ever counted by tens? Try it. It's pretty easy.

10, 20, 30, 40, 50, 60, 70, 80, 90, 100... Ready or not!

10
20
30
40
50
60
70
80
90
100

Look at the list. Do you notice anything interesting about it?

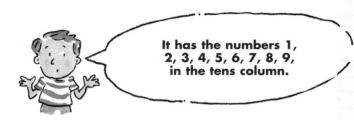

It has the numbers 1, 2, 3, 4, 5, 6, 7, 8, 9, in the tens column.

Yes, that's right. And what does it have in the ones column?

It has 0's in the ones column.

Right again. When we multiply any whole number by 10, it means we take that number ten times, and the amazing thing is that no matter what number we start with, we ALWAYS end up with that same starting number with a 0 at the end.

$$8 \times 10 = 80$$

$$37 \times 10 = 370$$

$$14 \times 10 = 140$$

$$650 \times 10 = 6500$$

Try a few numbers yourself.

The rule is that each time you multiply any whole number by 10, you put a 0 at the end of the number to get the answer.

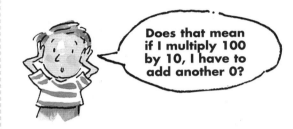

Does that mean if I multiply 100 by 10, I have to add another 0?

Yes! 100×10 means you have 100 ten times. That equals 1,000.

$$100 \times 10 = 1,000.$$

Now that you know how to multiply by 10, test your skill with The Hit the Jackpot Game on page 72.

The Hit the Jackpot Game

For two players or two teams. Starting with a 1 card, players multiply by 10 or 1 to make 1,000,000. The first side to make 1,000,000 wins the game.

How to Play

1 You need only 0 cards, 1 cards, and 10 cards for this game. Shuffle all the other cards and have each player or team draw a card. Highest card goes first.

2 Each player or team gets a 1 card to start with. Put it number-side-up in front of you.

3 Take the pile of eight 10's and put it together with six 1's. Shuffle them together well, then place them in the middle, number-side-down. This is the "multiplying" pile.

4 Place the pile of 0's where all players can reach it.

5 The first player picks a card from the "multiplying" pile and multiplies her starting 1 card by the number she picked. If she picked 1, her number doesn't change. If she picked 10, the player takes a 0 card from the 0 pile and adds it to the right end of her number.

6 The player returns the multiplying card to the middle pile by placing it, number-side-down, underneath the pile. And it's the second player's turn.

7 Take turns picking from the middle pile and multiplying your numbers accordingly. Keep playing until one player or team reaches 1,000,000.

NOTE: Multiplying by 1 DOES NOT change your number, because it tells you to take the number only one time:

$$1 \times 1 = 1$$

Multiplying by 10 DOES change your number, because it tells you to take your number ten times:

$$1 \times 10 = 10$$

Ten Does It Again!

Ten also makes it easy to divide.

Let's talk again about what dividing means. Dividing is breaking a number into equal-sized groups. To divide the number 8 by the number 2, ask yourself: How many groups of 2 each are in 8?

You get four equal groups of 2 each, so

8 ÷ 2 = 4

When you divide 20 by 10 ask: How many groups of 10 each are in 20?

There are two groups of 10 each in 20.

20 ÷ 10 = 2

Whenever the number has a zero at the end, it's easy to divide it into groups of 10. Try it with 50.

Guess how many groups of 10 are going to be in 50?

Five?

That's right:

♥ ♥ ♥ ♥ ♥ ♥ ♥ ♥ ♥ ♥
♥ ♥ ♥ ♥ ♥ ♥ ♥ ♥ ♥ ♥
♥ ♥ ♥ ♥ ♥ ♥ ♥ ♥ ♥ ♥
♥ ♥ ♥ ♥ ♥ ♥ ♥ ♥ ♥ ♥
♥ ♥ ♥ ♥ ♥ ♥ ♥ ♥ ♥ ♥

$$50 \div 10 = 5$$

Now try it with 100:

$$100 \div 10 = 10$$

Wait a minute. All you did was take a zero off the end of the number, and that was the answer!

You got it!!

$$40 \div 10 = \ \ 4$$
$$790 \div 10 = 79$$
$$100 \div 10 = 10$$
$$50 \div 10 = \ \ 5$$

When a number with a zero at the end is divided by 10, all you have to do is take away one zero from the end to find the answer.

The Going Bankrupt Game

For two players or teams. Starting with 1,000,000, players divide by 1 or 10 and try to keep their 1,000,000 from turning into 1.

How to Play

1 You will need only the 0's, 1's, and 10's from the card deck. Pull them out and stack each number in its own pile.

2 Use the leftover cards to decide which player starts the game. The player drawing the lowest card goes first.

3 Each player or team gets a 1 card and six 0 cards to start. Arrange them to make 1,000,000 in front of you. (You can use paper clips or other small items to make commas if you wish.)

4 Take six 10's and the remaining pile of six 1's and put them together. Shuffle them well. Place that pile in the middle, number-side-down. This is the "dividing" pile.

5 The first player picks a card from the center pile. The card will be either a 1 or a 10. Divide your starting 1,000,000 by the number you picked. If you picked 1, your number doesn't change (see Note). If you picked 10, take one 0 away from your number.

6 Place the 0's you have removed in a pile on the side.

7 Return the "dividing" card to the middle pile by placing it, number-side-down, underneath the pile.

8 Players take turns picking from the middle pile and dividing their numbers accordingly. The first player to lose all his 0's loses the game.

Note: Since dividing is taking a number and breaking it into equal groups, to divide by 1 you break the number into groups of 1 each. Take the number 5, for example. To divide 5 by 1 ($5 \div 1$), you make 5 into groups of one each:

You end up with five groups of one.

$$5 \div 1 = 5.$$

It's always like that. Whenever you divide any number by 1, the answer is always the exact same number you started with.

$$4 \div 1 = 4$$
$$13 \div 1 = 13$$
$$20 \div 1 = 20$$
$$100 \div 1 = 100$$

Why do you think it works that way?

The Number Grid Game

(for intermediate or advanced players)

For two players or two teams. Players or teams will need pencil and paper, and a pebble or other small marker. Players play on a five-square by five-square grid.

How to Play

1 Draw a five-square by five-square grid. Put an X in the middle box and a number in the corner of each of the squares except the X square. Starting in the upper left corner, number from 12 to 1 up to the X square, and then from 1 to 12 after the X square (see illustration). For more challenge, number the squares by 5's from 60 to 5, and from 5 to 60.

2 Remove the 0 cards from the deck and shuffle the remaining cards. Deal six cards to each player or team. These are your "equation cards" to use throughout the game. Lay them out number-side-up in front of you.

3 Each player picks a card from the deck. The lowest number goes first. Return the two cards to the deck. Place the deck, number-side-down, between the players.

4 The first player picks the top card and lays it number-side-up next to the pile. Starting at the X square, move the marker the number of squares indicated by the card. Moves may be made diagonally, up, down, or sideways. You may change direction as you move, but **you must move to a square that touches either a side or a corner of the square you are in.**

5 As they move, players MAY NOT cross through or land on the X square or backtrack squares through which they have already passed in that turn.

6 When the first player arrives at the destination square, he uses his cards to make an equation to equal the number of that square. Use as many cards as you can for this equation. Points are given for the number of cards used.

7 Write your equation in the square.

If it is correct, put your initial next to the number at the top of the square to CLAIM the square. Leave the marker in that square.

8 The second player picks a card from the deck. Starting from where the first player left the marker, the second player moves the number of squares indicated by the card.

9 When the second player lands on her square, she makes an equation with her cards to equal the number of the square. She writes her equation in the square. If it is correct, she adds her initial to CLAIM the square, and leaves her marker in that square.

10 Players MAY NOT move through squares claimed by their opponents. They MAY move only through their own squares and unclaimed squares.

11 Players continue to play back and forth. If a player picks a card and can't move that number of spaces, he forfeits his turn. If a player can't make the equation for her square she loses her turn. The marker stays at the previous square.

12 When all squares are claimed or when neither team can move the game is over. Each player adds up his score this way: the numbers at the top of your squares, plus the number of cards used to make your equation. For example, if on square 6 you made the equation $3+4-1$, you would get six points for the square plus three points for the cards—nine points in all. The player with the most points wins.

SQUARE 6 = 6
3 CARDS = 3 +
POINTS = 9